D1299514

Polish Americans

MARGARET C. HALL

Editorial Consultant:
Ann Hetzel Gunkel, Ph.D.

Heinemann Library
Chicago, Illinois

Created by the publishing team at Heinemann Library
Designed by Roslyn Broder
Photo Research by Amor Montes de Oca
Printed and Bound in the United States by Lake Book Manufacturing, Inc.

07 06 05 04 03
10 9 8 7 6 5 4 3 2 1

Library of Congress Cataloging-in-Publication Data
Hall, Margaret, 1947-
     Polish Americans / M.C. Hall.
        p. cm. — (We are America)
     Summary: Describes the conditions in Poland that led people
to immigrate to the United States and what their daily lives are
like in their new home.
     Includes bibliographical references (p.) and index.
     ISBN 1-40340-736-3 (lib. bdg.) ISBN 1-40343-137-X (pbk.)
     1. Polish Americans—Juvenile literature. 2. Immigrants—United
States—Juvenile literature. 3. United States—Emigration and
immigration—Juvenile literature. 4. Poland—Emigration and
immigration—Juvenile literature. 5. Polish Americans—Biography
—Juvenile literature. 6. Immigrants—United States—Biography
—Juvenile literature.   [1. Polish Americans.]   I. Title.   II. Series.
E184.P7H16 2003
973'.049185—dc21
                              2002013100

Acknowledgments
The author and publishers are grateful to the following for permission to reproduce copyright material:
pp. 4, 5, 28, 29 Courtesy of Ann Hetzel Gunkel; pp. 7, 8, 9, 14, 16 Hulton Archive/Getty Images; pp. 10, 13, 25 Bettmann/Corbis; p. 11 Chicago Daily News/Chicago Historical Society; p. 12 Bettman/Corbis; pp. 17, 21 Lewis Wickes Hine/Corbis; p. 18 Sandy Felsenthal/Corbis; pp. 19, 20 Courtesy of Calumet Regional Archive; p. 22 Bob Daemmrich/The Image Works; p. 23 Chicago Historical Society; p. 24 University of Chicago Special Collections; p. 26 Gino Domenico/AP Wide World Photos; p. 27 Kelly-Mooney Photography/Corbis

Cover photographs by (foreground) Robert Brenner/PhotoEdit, Inc., (background) Courtesy of The Polish Museum of America Photo Collection

For Ann Hetzel Gunkel and her son, Stanislaw, great-great grandson of Bernard and Wladyslawa Dankowski. Special thanks to Hedwig Ratajczak and Deloris Citterman for sharing memories of their grandparents.

Special thanks to Ann Hetzel Gunkel, Ph.D., professor of humanities and cultural studies at Columbia College, Chicago, and John Radzilowski of the University of Minnesota for their comments in preparation of this book.

Some quotations and material used in this book come from the following source. In some cases, quotes have been abridged for clarity: p. 15 *Writing Home: Immigrants in Brazil and the United States, 1890-1891* by Witold Kula (Bradenton, Fla.: Eastern European Monographs, 1987).

Every effort has been made to contact copyright holders of any material reproduced in this book. Any omissions will be rectified in subsequent printings if notice is given to the publisher.

Some words are shown in bold, **like this.** You can find out what they mean by looking in the glossary.

On the cover of this book, children dressed in traditional Polish costumes are shown. Milwaukee Avenue in Chicago, Illinois, a city with a large Polish-American population, is shown in the background in 1903.

Contents

One Family's Story

Bernard Dankowski was born in 1853 in western Poland. A year later, Wladyslawa Odorowska was born in the same town. When they grew up, Bernard and Wladyslawa got married. At that time, other countries controlled Poland.

This is Wladyslawa and Bernard Dankowski. Wladyslawa is pronounced like this: (vlad-ee-suav-ah).

Bernard knew that he might be forced to join another country's army. He decided to leave Poland and go to the United States.

Grandma told of when they were crossing the ocean they saw mermaids in the distance . . . They said they could see the flowing hair. Now [people] tell us they were only ugly **manatees.**

Hedwig Ratajczak, granddaughter of Bernard and Wladyslawa Dankowski, speaking about her grandmother's trip to the United States

In 1879, Bernard traveled by ship to New York City. First, he went to Detroit, Michigan. Then he moved to Minnesota, where he bought some farmland. Bernard soon went back to Poland. Like many Polish **immigrants,** Bernard had to leave his family back in Poland, and he missed them. In 1883, Bernard made his last trip to the United States. This time his wife and three young daughters came with him. One of the Dankowskis' daughters became sick and died during the trip. Another died soon after the family arrived in the United States.

Bernard and Wladyslawa's son Henry got married in Minnesota in about 1909. His wife was named Veronica Kruk.

Poland

In the late 1700s, soldiers from the countries of Russia, Prussia, and Austria marched into Poland. Soldiers from each country took control of part of Poland. The **Poles** fought to stay free, but by 1795, the rulers of Russia, Prussia, and Austria controlled all of Poland. Life changed for the Polish people. Teachers could not use the Polish language or teach Polish history. Instead, students had to study the language and history of the country that controlled that part of Poland.

Today, Prussia is not a nation. The land that was once called Prussia is now parts of Germany, Russia, and Poland.

This map shows where Poland and the United States are located in the world.

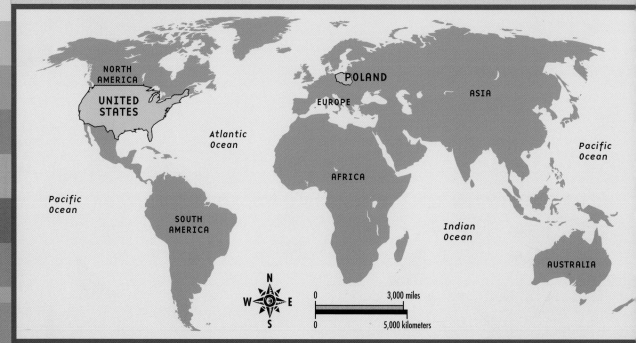

NORTH AMERICA

UNITED STATES

POLAND

EUROPE

ASIA

Atlantic Ocean

Pacific Ocean

Pacific Ocean

SOUTH AMERICA

AFRICA

Indian Ocean

AUSTRALIA

N W E S

0   3,000 miles

0   5,000 kilometers

Marie Curie, shown in a laboratory in about 1910, also discovered an element called radium. She was born in Poland in 1867 near Warsaw.

Even after losing their **independence,** the Polish people held on to their **culture.** They started secret schools where children and adults could learn Poland's history and language. There was even a secret college. It was called the Flying University because classes met in a different place every week.

Marie Curie went to the Flying University. She and her husband, Pierre, made many scientific discoveries. They named one **element** they discovered *polonium,* for Poland. Before she was married, Marie Curie's name was Maria Sklodowska.

The First Polish Immigrants

In 1607, English **settlers** founded the Jamestown **colony** in what is now the state of Virginia. Soon after they arrived, they had to build houses, dig wells, and farm the land. A group of Polish men who also came to Jamestown helped the English settlers.

This painting shows what it might have looked like when settlers were building Jamestown. Jamestown was the first English settlement in America.

*Polish **immigrants** might have helped to make bricks at Jamestown, like the person in the painting above is doing. Bricks were needed to build houses and other buildings.*

The Jamestown colony belonged to England. In 1619, the government of England allowed the Jamestown colonists to choose their own leaders. Only the English colonists could vote for these leaders. The Poles refused to work until they were given the same right.

The first **Poles** arrived in Jamestown in 1608. They cleared land for farming, built homes, and set up workshops. They opened a factory to make glass. Polish workers also made other things the colonists needed, such as soap and tar.

Immigration Continues

In about 1775, a different group of **Poles** came to America. They were men who had been fighting for Poland's **independence.** They heard that many **colonists** did not want to be controlled by Great Britain anymore. They believed in independence so much that they decided to help the colonists fight the **Revolutionary War.**

Thaddeus Kosciuszko and Casimir Pulaski were two Poles who joined George Washington's army in the Revolutionary War. American historians call these men heroes because of the help they gave to the colonists.

This painting shows Thaddeus Kosciuszko, a Polish soldier who helped American soldiers win the Revolutionary War.

Some Polish children attended schools like this one in Chicago, Illinois, shown in the early 1900s.

Time Line

1608	Skilled Polish workers arrive in Jamestown.
1772–1795	Poland loses its independence. Some Poles leave Poland for the United States.
1776–1783	Poles help fight the Revolutionary War.
1830	About 400 Poles escape to the U.S. after an unsuccessful fight for independence in Poland.
1854	About 100 immigrant families start the first Polish community in the U.S. at Panna Maria, Texas.
1870–1914	More than two million Polish immigrants come to the U.S.
1921	A law limits the number of Polish **immigrants** who can enter the U.S.
1921–2000	More than 600,000 Polish immigrants come to the U.S.

During the 1850s, other Polish **immigrants** came to the United States. Some worked on farms in the Northeast. Others came in groups of 50 to 100 families to start their own farming towns in the Midwest and in Texas. Some Polish immigrants joined the **pioneers** who **settled** the West or searched for gold in California.

Leaving Poland

Life was hard in Poland during the 19th century. Some **Poles** owned their land. However, most were **peasants** who rented their farms from rich landowners. They worked long hours to grow their crops. They had to sell much of what they grew just to pay their rent. The population of Poland was growing quickly at this time. There was not enough land to support all the people.

*These Polish women came to the United States in about 1910. They are shown at Ellis Island, a center for new **immigrants** that used to operate in New York.*

Another reason that Polish people came to the United States was to escape danger. In 1920, these Polish immigrants went to Germany to take ships to the United States. At the time, Poland was at war with Russia.

Many men left their villages to find work in large cities. Women earned money by sewing and washing clothes for other people. Some men decided they would be better off going to the United States. They knew that American factories needed workers. Many of them planned to save money and return to Poland to buy land of their own.

Coming to America

For many **Poles,** the trip to the United States was the first time they had ever left their villages. They took trains to **ports** in Germany where ships were leaving for the United States. By 1870, most ships were powered by steam engines. A trip that had taken months now took two to three weeks. Still, it was a hard journey. In bad weather, travelers crowded together below the decks. This made it easy for sickness to spread. Some travelers died before they reached the United States.

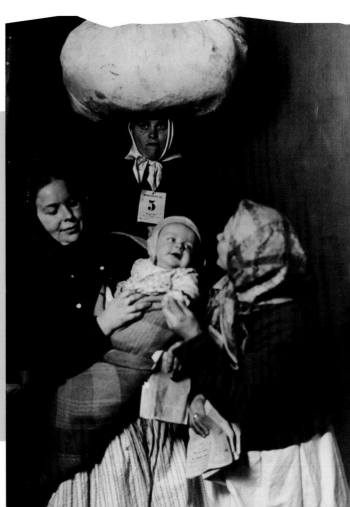

These European immigrants came to the United States in 1905. The woman in the back has her possessions in a large bag that is balanced on her head.

Polish Immigration to the United States

This map shows the areas in the United States where many Polish people first moved to and where many Polish Americans live today.

Polish **immigrants** entered the United States at large port cities such as New York, Philadelphia, and Hoboken, New Jersey. Many moved on to cities in the Northeast or Midwest. They usually moved to be close to family members who were already in the country.

> Take with you two cooked geese . . . a few ducks or roasted chickens, and about two loaves of brown bread because on the ocean liner you will not be able to eat that which they give you.
>
> —Stanislaus Kazmirkiewicz, in a letter to family members planning to come to the U.S. from Poland

New Jobs

More than two million Polish **immigrants** came to the United States between 1870 and 1914. Most of them had been farmers in Poland. But they did not have enough money to buy land in the United States.

In the late 1800s, factories were very important in the United States. There were factories for making steel, **textile mills** for making cloth, and **slaughterhouses** where workers cut up meat. After 1900, there were also factories where cars were made.

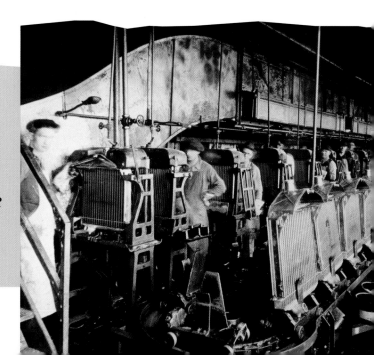

Some Polish immigrants worked in factories like this one, shown in 1915, where car parts were made.

Polish women worked long hours in shops like this one in New York City, seen in 1908. Workers there made men's clothing.

Most Polish immigrants found jobs in factories, mills, and mines. They worked long hours at dangerous jobs. Immigrant workers were sometimes injured or killed because the places they worked in were unsafe. Still, even children and women found jobs. Young boys worked in coal mines. Women and children worked in textile mills.

Between 1880 and 1900, about 36,000 Polish immigrants worked in coal mines in Pennsylvania. In September 1897, a group of miners in Lattimer, Pennsylvania, marched to demand safer places to work. Local police officers shot at the group. Most of the 19 workers who were killed were Polish.

Polish-American Communities

Many Polish **immigrants** only wanted to stay in the United States long enough to earn money to buy land in Poland. So they tried to save money and live like they had in Poland. They lived together in neighborhoods that were like Polish villages. Stores sold **traditional** Polish foods. Newspapers were printed in the Polish language.

Many Polish immigrants did not stay in the United States. Of every three Polish immigrants who came to the United States between 1906 and 1914, one went back to Poland.

This photo shows Milwaukee Avenue in Chicago, a large street in an area of Chicago where many Polish Americans live.

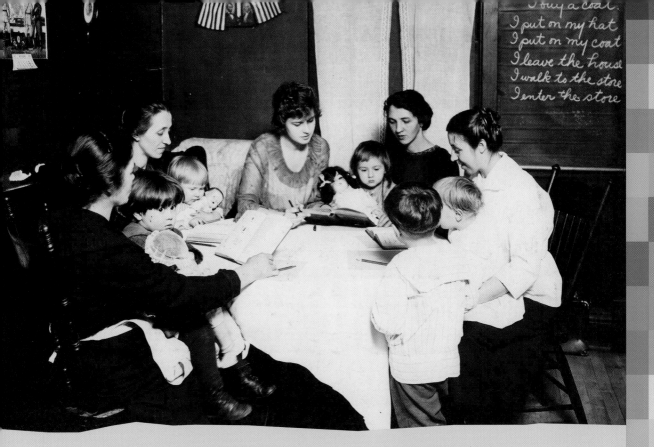

These women belonged to a group in Gary, Indiana, that held dances and other activities where Poles could meet one another. The group was called the International Institute.

The **Poles** who decided to stay in the United States bought homes and businesses. They gave money to build churches and schools in their neighborhoods. Polish Americans formed groups to keep their language and traditions alive. The groups helped the Poles hold on to their **culture** and feel less separated from family members back in Poland.

Polish immigrants called their neighborhood communities *Polonia.* The word means "Polish America."

Homes

Some **immigrants** rented houses that belonged to companies they worked for. Often, these houses had only one room. The roof might have leaked and the walls barely kept out the cold. Polish-American families saved as much money as they could. With the money they saved, many families bought houses. Some families then took in **boarders** to earn extra money. The boarders paid for a room and meals.

In 1918, immigrant workers lived in this building, which was in a Polish-American neighborhood in Gary, Indiana. The area was known as Shacktown at the time.

In the early 1900s, family members who worked in factories or mills often lived in the same small houses. This photo from 1912 shows members of a family that worked in a mill.

Polish-American women were proud of their homes. They worked hard to keep everything clean. Whenever they had the space, they planted gardens and grew flowers. They also grew vegetables, such as cabbage and potatoes. They used what they grew to feed their families.

Church and School

Most of the Polish **immigrants** who came to the United States between 1870 and 1914 were **Catholic.** The local church was a very important part of their lives. Polish Americans gave money to build large, beautiful churches. These churches were symbols of pride in the community. Many Polish **Jews** also went to the United States before **World War One.** They went to find jobs and to escape unfair treatment.

This church was built in 1882 by Polish Americans in Panna Maria, Texas.

This Polish-American man owned a shop in Chicago that sold items that people used in churches, such as candles and prayer books.

Polish Americans also built Catholic schools. At first, classes were taught in Polish. Many children only went to school until the sixth grade. Then they went to work. They sold newspapers, worked in family stores, or took jobs in factories or **textile mills.** They gave most of what they earned to their parents.

Culture and Traditions

Polish Americans enjoyed getting together to share their **culture.** Clubs met to listen to music by Frédéric Chopin and other Polish **composers.** They also performed **traditional**

The **Pole** listening to Chopin listens to the voice of his whole race.
—Ignacy Paderewski, Polish pianist

Polish dances, such as the mazurka and the polonaise. People borrowed books printed in Polish from libraries. They formed **literary circles** to discuss books by Polish writers.

This group of children is shown performing traditional Polish dances.

These Polish children are shown on a ship that came to the United States in 1948. They moved from Poland to Detroit, Michigan.

In their neighborhoods, Polish Americans knew one another well. Parents watched their own children and their neighbors' children. On Sunday mornings, everyone went to church. On Sunday afternoons, they visited friends and relatives. They talked, played cards, and worked on household chores together.

Polish Americans showed great love for their new land. When the U.S. entered **World War Two** in 1941, the army needed soldiers. Many Polish Americans were among the first 100,000 who joined the army.

Celebrations

Easter is one of the most important Polish-American holidays. Families come together to share big meals. They eat **traditional** foods, such as hard-boiled eggs,

Beet salad is served at traditional Polish-American Easter meals. It is made with cooked beets, lemon juice, salt, and sugar.

sausage, and *babka,* a sweet bread. People paint beautiful designs on eggs to use as decorations.

These women wore traditional Polish clothing to march in the Pulaski Day Parade in New York City.

In 1992, these girls performed with a Polish-American group called the Matusz Polish Dance Circle. The group danced as part of the Polish Festival held in Holmdel, New Jersey.

Pulaski Day is a Polish-American holiday. There are parades to honor Casimir Pulaski, who fought beside the Americans during the **Revolutionary War.** Polish Americans also celebrate with Polish music and dances. Some people wear traditional clothing for these events. The clothing is often red and white, which are the colors of Poland's flag.

The Dankowskis' Story Continues

This is a family photo taken the day Bernard and Wladyslawa's son Kasper got married in about 1911.

At first, Bernard and Wladyslawa Dankowski lived in Pittsburgh, Pennsylvania. Bernard worked as a baker to earn money to take care of his family. In 1888, the Dankowskis moved to southwestern Minnesota. They planned to farm the land Bernard had bought in the small town of Wilno. Like many other Polish Americans, Bernard worked hard to make life in the United States just how he dreamed it would be.

Bernard built a house for his family. During the winter, he went back to Pittsburgh to earn money as a baker. In the spring, he worked on the farm. After a few years, Bernard was able to stay in Minnesota all year long. He and Wladyslawa lived on their farm until they both died in 1942. Their granddaughter, Frances Ratajczak, now lives on the Dankowski land.

This is a photo of Beverly, Florence, and Bruce Dankowski. They are the grandchild and great-grandchildren of Bernard and Wladyslawa.

Polish Immigration Chart

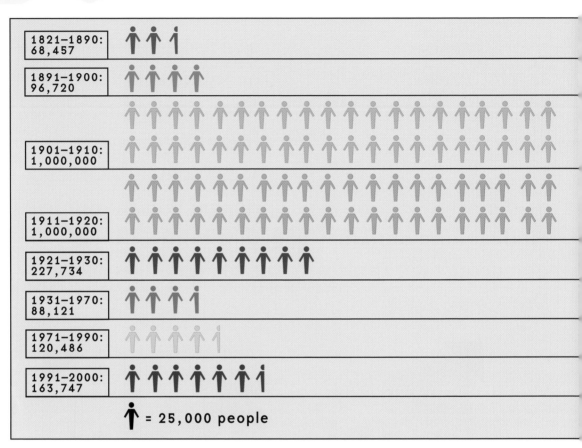

Period	Immigration
1821–1890: 68,457	
1891–1900: 96,720	
1901–1910: 1,000,000	
1911–1920: 1,000,000	
1921–1930: 227,734	
1931–1970: 88,121	
1971–1990: 120,486	
1991–2000: 163,747	

= 25,000 people

The figures for 1901 to 1920 are guesses. Because Poland was not **independent** *during those years, most Polish* **immigrants** *were listed as coming from another country.*

Source: U.S. Immigration and Naturalization Service

More Books to Read

Kapowski, Samuel. *I Am Polish American.* New York: Rosen Publishing, 1998.

Raatma, Lucia. *Polish Americans.* Chanhassen, Minn.: The Child's World, 2002.

Wallner, Rosemary, and John Radzilowski. *Polish Immigrants, 1890-1920.* Mankato, Minn.: Capstone Press, 2002.

Glossary

boarder person who pays for meals and a place to sleep in someone's home

Catholic member of the Roman Catholic Church, the religion led by the pope that follows teachings of the Bible

colony territory that is owned or ruled by another country

composer someone who writes music for others to sing or play

culture ideas, skills, arts, and way of life for a certain group of people

element substance that cannot be separated into different substances. Gold and carbon are elements.

immigrate to come to a country to live there for a long time. A person who immigrates is an immigrant.

independent condition of being free from the rule of other countries, governments, or people. The state of being independent is called independence.

Jew person who follows the Jewish religion or has Jewish ancestors

literary circle group that meets to discuss books and other written works

manatee large mammal that lives in water. It has flippers and a broad, flat tail.

peasant poor, uneducated person who usually survives by farming

pioneer person who is one of the first to move to a new place

Pole person who was born or who lives in Poland or has Polish ancestors

port city near water where ships dock and leave from

Revolutionary War war from 1775 to 1783 between the thirteen American colonies and Great Britain

settle to make a home for yourself and others

slaughterhouse factory in which animals are killed and prepared as meat

textile mill factory where cloth and thread are made

tradition belief or practice handed down through the years from one generation to the next

World War One first worldwide war in which many countries took sides to fight against each other

World War Two war fought from 1939 to 1945 by Germany, Japan, and Italy on one side and the United States, Great Britain, China, Poland, France, and the Soviet Union on the other

Index